NOTTINGHAMS PRIVIES

by

DAVID BELL

COUNTRYSIDE BOOKS

NEWBURY · BERKSHIRE

COUNTRYSIDE BOOKS
3 Catherine Road
Newbury, Berkshire

ISBN 1 85306 591 9

*For Lee Stone, a computer wizard,
who has rescued me again and again.*

Produced through MRM Associates Ltd., Reading
Typeset by Techniset Typesetters, Merseyside
Printed by Woolnough Bookbinding Ltd., Irthlingborough

CONTENTS

The author checking out a three-holer privy seat at Keyworth.

FOREWORD

Most of the information in this book came in letters and telephone calls from Nottinghamshire residents in response to my broadcast on Nick Brunger's afternoon show on Radio Nottingham, and my letters in local newspapers. People from Huthwaite to Newark, from Keyworth to Sturton-le-Steeple, sent me their reminiscences. Some were thankful that the gruesome days of the ashpit privy were over. Others were most nostalgic for the days when you could go down the garden and sit in the privy with the door wide open, smoking a pipe and contemplating the view. Some sent me poems on the subject, others sent me tales that had me laughing fit to burst. Many invited me over to their cottage or farm, their stately home and, on one occasion, even a Bishop's palace, to take a look at their old privy.

Frequently these generous people supplied me with cups of tea and biscuits, and everyone wanted to discuss my project. Most of them understood my fascination with the subject, though one or two asked 'Why on earth are you interested in privies?' My response to the question varied. My flippant answer was that I had always been 'round the bend' or that I was 'flushed with pride' due to my previous book on the subject. My more serious answer was that the story of the privy is an important part of our social history, and that, as the people who can remember it are getting fewer in number as the years roll on, it is essential that their memories are put on record now.

Everyone agreed that the project was worthwhile. Going to the loo is such a universal need – dukes and dustmen, bishops and bus-drivers, they all have to go – that the privy can be seen as the most democratic of institutions. It is the great leveller. As I was told, if your boss is giving you a hard time, picturing him sitting on his privy helps put him into perspective. It is the one place where it is impossible to be pompous!

It is perhaps necessary, as my old English teacher was wont to say, to define one's terms. What is a privy? The *Shorter Oxford Dictionary* defines it as 'a lavatory, especially an outside one or one without plumbing'. So I have, on the whole, used the word to mean an outside lavatory where the sewage is collected either in an ashpit below the privy or in a bucket (which in Nottinghamshire is often called a 'mucktub'). I have also investigated the garderobe – an indoor privy found in castles and stately homes – and the much later outdoor WC, a flushing privy usually connected to the sewage system (and much given to freezing up in winter).

I owe many debts of gratitude to the many people who helped with my researches (see Acknowledgements), but I would like to place on record my particular thanks to my wife Rosemary for patiently putting up with me returning from the wilds of rural Notts with enthusiastic cries of 'I've got a photo of a privy ash mechanism!' or 'I've found a four-holer at last!'

DAVID BELL

[1]

A Quick Trot through the History of the Privy

The earliest privies were simply a hole in the ground, and are described by Moses in the Book of Deuteronomy (see Literature and Legends). A hole that could be used once, then covered over and left was an ideal latrine for a nomadic tribe, but when people began to settle in one place, something a little more permanent was needed. The hole would have to be larger – a pit which could be used over a period of time. Add four walls for privacy, and a seat for real luxury, and what you have is a privy that any resident of Nottinghamshire between the Middle Ages and the early 1900s would recognise.

The earliest Nottinghamshire privies were built over an ashpit, because it was found that throwing ash, dry soil or sand onto the waste made it more pleasant, covering it and absorbing the wetness. Other household refuse was also thrown in, as this was an easy means of disposal. As a boy, Peter Hammond of West Bridgford began collecting broken clay pipes from the fields around his home. 'It was only later I found out how they had got there,' he told me. 'They had been thrown into privy ashpits along with broken crockery, then collected with the nightsoil and spread on the fields as manure!'

Later the old pits below the privies were filled in, and large buckets – always known in Nottinghamshire as muck tubs – replaced them. The only snag now was that, while ashpits only needed emptying once or twice a year, the muck tubs had to be emptied every week. At first, the bucket privies had to be emptied by lifting the seat to get to the tub underneath, but later privies had a small door at the back, by which the bucket could be

A privy bucket – or muck tub – had to be sturdy and capacious with two firm carrying handles.

Newark Castle ruins.

removed without going into the privy itself. Of course, this had its own possible snags. One lady told me that she was in her privy, when the bucket was removed from under her. 'I heard this rattle and felt this draught,' she told me, 'and then the bucket had gone!' She had forgotten it was the day for the night-soil men to call.

The preferred place for getting rid of privy dung was the local river, which would take it away. The fact that people living downstream would inherit it from you was their problem, not yours. This wasn't just an anti-social habit of the worker in his cottage; it was the accepted practice for those who lived in castles too. The indoor privies found in castles were called garderobes, and were often placed in the castle walls, so that the waste would fall directly into the river or the moat. A river was preferable since the ordure would be immediately conveyed out of sight,

9

and even more importantly out of smelling range. The stagnant water of a moat was a less agreeable method of disposal, and must have stunk to high heaven. I can just imagine medieval soldiers ordered to attack a castle, saying to their commander, 'I don't mind facing the boiling oil and the arrows, but there's no way I'm wading through that moat!'

Sometimes the garderobes were corbelled out so that they were suspended over the river, but in other castles the waste would fall through a chute or chimney and emerge at the foot of the wall. This was the case at Newark Castle, where an outlet for the garderobes can be seen at the bottom of a tower on the edge of the River Trent.

Actually the word garderobe literally means a wardrobe, and originally described a chamber where clothing was hung. This chamber often had a privy leading off it, and the word became used for the privy itself. While we might smile at the people of the Middle Ages using a euphemism for the privy, we ought to remember that we do exactly the same ourselves. When we ask 'Would you like to use the cloakroom?' this is our precise equivalent. Most of our words for the privy are euphemisms. Both a lavatory and a toilet meant a place for washing right up until Victorian times. In a Victorian catalogue of sanitary fittings, all the references to lavatories are accompanied by illustrations of what we would call a washbasin!

Not all castles and stately homes had garderobes where the waste fell into a chamber beneath or into a passing river. Some were simply small rooms that housed a close stool; these were chamber pots concealed in a elaborate chair, in principle very like the Victorian commode. Close stools could be highly decorated, and look exactly like a royal throne. Indeed King Louis XIV frequently received foreign ambassadors and conducted affairs of state while sitting on his close stool.

Nottinghamshire, like the rest of the country, used the privy throughout the centuries, until the great inventors of the late 18th century came to the rescue. Great pioneers in this field included Alexander Cummings and Joseph Bramah who began to develop the water closet with patents taken out in 1775 and 1778 respectively. Strangely enough, it is the name of a later inventor – Thomas Crapper – who caught the attention of the public. It is not difficult to see why. Crapper has joined that illustrious band – Hoover, Bloomer, Sandwich, Wellington and so on – who have given a new word to the English language.

Thomas Crapper was a true Victorian being born in 1837, the year that Queen Victoria came to the throne. At the age of eleven, he left his native Yorkshire and walked – via Nottinghamshire – to London to seek his fortune. He found work as an apprentice plumber in Chelsea, and was able to set up his own sanitary engineering company at the age of twenty-four. It was a good time to do so. London was just about to build over eighty miles of sewers.

Crapper's great invention was the Water Waste Preventer. This stopped people tying down the water chain in order to have a continuous flow of water through their lavatory bowls. He invented the siphon and chain flushing system that many of us remember. He was very thorough in testing his invention. In his workshop he had a test panel of five toilets fed from a huge 200 gallon water-tank on the roof. The simulated contents of the toilet bowl included smudge, otherwise known as plumber's grease, plus sponges, apples, cotton waste and what he called air vessels – these were paper bags filled with air. To pass Crapper's rigorous standards, his flush had to remove all these objects. In 1884, he recorded that one single flush had disposed of a quantity of smudge smeared on the pan, with four pieces of paper adhering to it, plus three air vessels, one sponge and ten apples! A delighted workman threw his cloth cap after the mixture, and that too was borne away by the flush.

THOS. CRAPPER & Co., Ltd.,

SANITARY ENGINEERS

TO

His Majesty the King.

AND

H.R.H. the Prince of Wales.

BY APPOINTMENT.

BY APPOINTMENT

BATHS, LAVATORIES, SINKS, &c

Show Rooms:

120, KING'S ROAD,

(Opposite Royal Avenue)

CHELSEA, S.W.

Thomas Crapper opened showrooms in Chelsea.

Single-seater privy at the Old Rectory, Bilsthorpe, complete with handle for the ash mechanism.

Thomas Crapper's name began to appear on sanitary porcelain, and it was during World War I that American servicemen based in England began to notice this appellation and say, 'I'm going to the Crapper!' This soon degenerated into: 'I'm going for a crap!' The word went back to the USA with the men, and later returned to Britain as a slang term for faeces initially, then as a general term for rubbish or nonsense.

It would appear, then, that the use of the ashpit privy went on from earliest times right up until the days of Bramah, Cummings and Crapper. However, that belief would ignore the work of a remarkable Elizabethan man, whose name deserves far more recognition that it ever gets. One of the major figures in the development of the flushing privy was Sir John Harington, the godson of Queen Elizabeth I. He designed England's very first

13

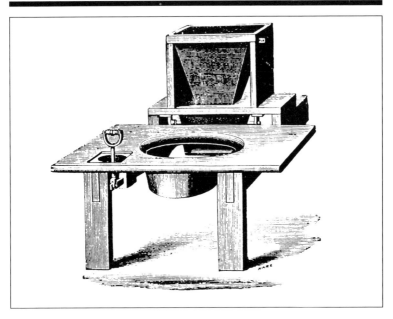

Moule's Patent Earth System. The ash was placed in the hopper and a measured amount was released when the handle was pulled. See page 16.

flushing lavatory, which he named 'The Mighty Ajax'. This title was, in fact, a pun on the Elizabethan term for a privy – a jakes. If the humour seems a little stretched to us, just imagine what future generations will make of our own puns and wordplay.

John Harington was a witty courtier and writer of plays and poetry, but sometimes his wit got him into trouble. He is the man who wrote those dangerously true words:

> Treason never prospers, and here's the reason
> For if it prospers, none dare call it treason.

His rather saucy translations of Italian verses caused his god-

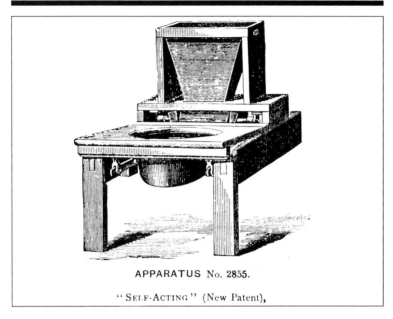

APPARATUS No. 2855.

" SELF-ACTING " (New Patent),

This version worked automatically when the user stood up!

mother to banish him from court on several occasions, but she was fond of him – referring to him as 'that witty fellow, my godson' – and always allowed him to return. John had an Ajax constructed at his home in the West Country, and wrote a book about it which he titled *The Metamorphosis of Ajax*. We know that is cost 30s 6d to build, but the name of the man who built it for him has been lost to history. All we have are his initials: T. C. The book caused John Harington more trouble, because he couldn't resist putting in a cheeky rhyme about a priest accidentally invoking the devil by praying while sitting on the privy. He also included a supernatural character called Captain Ajax who would, if provoked, cause the sitter to suffer from diarrhoea!

Despite his light-hearted approach to the subject, the inven-

15

tion of the Ajax was a very practical one. Not only did Haring-ton describe and illustrate his invention, he built two of them. One was installed at his own home, and Queen Elizabeth commissioned the other to be installed at Richmond Palace. Her subjects, however, regarded the flushing privy as another one of the Queen's eccentricities. She was said to be obsessed with personal hygiene, and it was whispered – though no-one could really credit it – that she 'bathed once a month whether she needed it or not!' This new-fangled idea was not to be taken seriously and everyone continued to use the ashpit privies for another two or three hundred years. That is why the name of the genuine pioneer – Harington – is hardly known, while that of Crapper is celebrated all over the world. It was not until the reign of a later queen – Victoria – that royal patronage was restored to the loo, when her consort, Prince Albert, persuaded her to install a flushing water closet in Windsor Castle.

Despite the popularity of the WC, many people remained faithful to the old-fashioned privy (indeed a number of Nottinghamshire people are still using them today). Those wonderful Victorian inventors did not ignore their needs, and came up with a cinder sifter to separate ash from cinders, and a privy that used the ash to cover the waste when a lever was pulled. I discovered a privy of this sort in the Old Rectory at Bilsthorpe. Another invention – the Automatic Earth Closet – even made the pulling of a handle unnecessary. When the user stood up, the ash would automatically descend onto the waste. There was a similar invention for a self-acting water closet, where the system flushed when the user stood up after using the WC.

[2]

STATELY HOMES, COUNTRY COTTAGES AND A BISHOP'S PALACE

During my researches into Nottinghamshire privies, I was fortunate enough to be invited to some of the county's grander residences. One of these was Holme Pierrepont Hall, situated a few miles east of Nottingham, close to the famous Holme Pierrepont National Water Sports Centre where our Olympic canoeists train. (Incidentally, it is Pierrepont, meaning stone bridge, not Pierrepoint like the hangman!) Holme Pierrepont Hall was built in the 16th century and is one of the earliest examples of building in brick. The present owners are Mr and Mrs Robin Brackenbury who generously allowed me to visit their home. Their son Robert showed me a ground floor garderobe – an indoor privy – situated to the west of the main entrance. It was actually a chamber that would have housed a close stool, which servants would have emptied each day. Robert Brackenbury informed me that there was another garderobe in the room to the east of the entrance, and others in the rooms above. From outside the Hall, it is possible to see a narrow vertical aperture in the wall, which formed the window – unglazed of course – of the second storey garderobe.

I also went to Wollaton Hall, but here I was visiting Nottingham's Industrial Museum. In particular, I was aiming for the outdoor display area where one of the city's street urinals was preserved. Robert Cox, the Keeper of Industry, accompanied me and allowed me to photograph it. He was also able to supply me with photographs of the urinal taken in 1973, when it stood on London Road, by the canal. There are no prizes for guessing where the waste water drained to!

17

The privy tower at the Bishop's Palace, Southwell.

Robert Brackenbury stands by the entrance to one of the ground floor garderobes at Holme Pierrepont Hall.

19

The urinal in its original situation by the canal, on London Road, Nottingham, in 1973. (Photo courtesy of Nottingham Industrial Museum)

Ashbox – complete with the original ash – on the privy at the Old Rectory, Bilsthorpe.

Another museum I went to was the Framework Knitters' Museum at Ruddington, where there are two well-preserved privies side by side. The nightsoil from these used to fall via a chute or chimney into a lower chamber behind the privies.

When I visited the Old Rectory at Bilsthorpe, I was shown a one-holer privy. I noticed that next to the normal hole where the user would sit, there was a small circular hole in the seat. It was about four inches in diameter, and situated by the right hand of anyone sitting on the privy. When Paula Panayi, the owner of the Old Rectory, said, 'There's a handle that fits in the little hole. I think I can find it for you,' I began to hold my breath in suppressed excitement. Sure enough, when Paula brought in a handle and fitted it in the hole, I could see that this privy had an ash mechanism. When the user had finished he would pull

21

This three-holer privy at Saundby is for two adults and a child.

the handle in the seat, releasing a quantity of ash or sand to cover the contents of the privy bucket. The ash box was still on the wall above the privy. When I looked into it, I was astounded – and delighted – to see that it was still half full of ash that must have been put in decades ago when the privy was still in use. I had once seen an illustration of a privy of this sort described in a Victorian catalogue of sanitary fittings, but now I had actually met one *in situ*. Thanks, Paula!

Also in Bilsthorpe I visited Inkersall Farm, where I was pleased to find a two-holer in a row of outbuildings. Like many two-hole privies, one of its holes was smaller and lower, obviously intended for the use of children. This was also the arrangement at a privy I saw in Besthorpe, although here the building was detached and brick-built with a pantile roof and a brick floor.

I managed to uncover one hole of this three-seater privy at Bevercotes. A second hole is under the cupboard on the left.

David Otter, Churchwarden, outside the privy block of the old school at Cotham.

However, the two-holer I visited at Sturton-le-Steeple, in the north-east of the county had two adult-sized holes, with an unusual narrow rectangular hole between them. This hole had a lid, and my guess is that it might have been for shovelling ash on top of the sewage in the pit below. Not far from Sturton, is the village

One of the three privies at the old school, Cotham. Judging by the step, this one was for the infants.

of Saundby, and there I visited the home of Madge and Robin Fletcher. In a corner of a yard that had not been changed for 200 years was the privy, and this one contained a three-holer! Again one of the holes was child-sized, the other two being for adults.

At Church Farm in Bevercotes, the privy had once contained three adult-sized holes, but was now used for storage of furniture, engine parts, glass and so on. Half an hour of clearing did manage to reveal the top of one hole, and I was interested to discover that it was an unusual shape, not a perfect circle but one which came to a point at the front. I was intrigued to hear from the owner, David Cheetham, that the farm had once boasted this three-hole privy plus a two-holer in another outbuilding. I can only speculate why the place should have needed so many privies. Perhaps the farm employed a large number of workers at one time. Or maybe they all lived on prunes, which a former headmistress of my acquaintance used to call 'the black-coated workers'!

I also visited the old school at Cotham, now used as an Anglican church every Sunday and a village hall during the week. Outside there were three separate privies, one for boys, one for girls, and the other for 'mixed infants'. The latter had a small wooden step up to the privy. I was delighted to find that the privies still had their internal fittings, especially when Mr Otter, the Churchwarden, told me that one of them was still used when social events took place there.

I had found privies in Nottinghamshire with one, two and even three holes, but did not expect to find one with four. However, I heard that there was something interesting in the grounds of Southwell Minster, Nottinghamshire's cathedral. I wrote to the Right Rev Patrick Harris, the Bishop of Southwell, who replied saying that I was welcome to come and look at the ruins of the old Bishop's Palace, which were in the grounds of his private gardens. The Bishop's Palace was built in the 14th and early

26

15th century, originally for the use of the Archbishop of York. However, it became uninhabitable in 1646, and eventually fell into ruin. In 1891, Bishop Trollope of Nottingham bought the palace ruins and gardens for £1,600. After restoring the old Court Room, he gave the property to the Bishopric of Southwell, in the hope that it would become the official residence of the Bishop of Southwell. The Bishop's Manor, the residence of the present Bishop, was built in the grounds of the Old Palace in 1905.

Most visitors come to the Bishop's Palace to see the old Court Room with its stained glass windows, but what I had come to see was a set of privies, in a small tower. I climbed the winding stone staircase, and at the top I found four privies set at right angles to each other, and situated over a deep, well-shaped pit. Only the wooden seats were missing. It was quite easy to imagine four 15th-century clerics sitting there, perhaps talking to each other – or even singing hymns in close harmony! However, these privies were not really as communal as the three-holers I had seen elsewhere, because each one was hidden from its neighbour by a stone partition. A set of steps leading downwards ended in a chamber below ground level. Once or twice a year, servants would be sent down to shovel out the nightsoil that had accumulated there. I imagine that it would not be the most eagerly awaited of their chores.

[3]

RURAL REMINISCENCES

Mrs Mabel Barber of Newark tells me that although a bucket and spade bring back happy memories for many people, this is not true for her. The mention of a bucket and spade makes her remember 1929 when her family was living in a cottage on the edge of the village of Winthorpe. Her mother, Mrs Osborne, had the onerous task of bringing up four children alone, so they all had to pitch in and help with the chores: chopping sticks, filling the oil lamps and keeping the side boiler topped up with water from the water butt. These were all done willingly, part of everyday life. However, the job the children all hated was having to empty the privy bucket every Saturday.

The three eldest children, Jessie aged 12, Mabel aged 11, and Ronald aged 9, used to take it in turns to dig a three-foot hole in the garden. This was very hard work, and used to take them over an hour. Then came the part they dreaded. They had to extricate the bucket from the back of the privy, all the while remembering to heed their mother's warning to 'Watch out for rats!' Mabel said that she never understood how any self-respecting rat could live in such a place. Taking the bucket to the hole was hazardous; it was far too heavy for the children to carry, so they had to drag it across the garden. Mabel says that they were grateful for the fact that the pieces of newspaper floated on the top, thus hiding the obnoxious contents.

Once they got it to the hole – which was somehow never quite big enough – they had to tip it up. Mabel admits that she always used to stand well back, behind her brother and sister, to avoid getting splashed. Then big sister Jessie would shovel soil back into the hole, while Mabel and Ronald washed and disinfected

A pair of outside bucket-privies at Bridge Cottages, Newark.

the bucket before returning it to its place in the privy.

Mabel recalls that it was frequently difficult to get the soil back into the hole, and sometimes they didn't make a very good job of it. Once, the neighbour's dog came tearing across the garden and fell in the hole. Jessie, being made of sterner stuff than Mabel, grabbed it by the collar and hauled it out. It ran round and round the garden in a frenzy before rushing back home. When it ran into the house, there was a terrible scream from its owner. Mabel doesn't know who cleaned the dog up, but she says that the friendly neighbours were somewhat less friendly for a while.

Every season had its own problems. Winter was the very worst time, because of the difficulty in digging the hole in frozen soil, but autumn was a bad time too. Every September, thousands of wasps occupied the pear tree growing near the privy. The children were frequently stung while completing their privy-empty-ing chore, and then out would come the blue bag. This was the bag of soda, chalk and ultramarine pigment used in the washing to make the whites whiter, and reputed to be the best thing for stings. 'I wonder if it did any good,' Mabel muses doubtfully.

The three continued with their Saturday bucket-and-spade work until 1938 when the family moved house. One thing that did annoy Mabel – and I suspect it still does – was that her youngest sister Janet was never expected to help with the task.

Mrs Peggy Bristow of Collingham says that as a girl she lived with her family in Coventry, but used to spend her school holi-days with her grandmother, Mrs Hopkinson, who lived in Besthorpe. About 30 feet from the house there was a brick-built privy surrounded by sycamore trees. The privy – known as the House of Lords – had a pantile roof and brick floor. Inside it had a two-holer seat, one hole being adult sized and the other a smaller one for children. Squares of newspaper hung from the nail in the wall, but for reading purposes there were a few copies of *Blackwood's Magazine* and a 3-foot-high pile of *The Lady's Companion* dating back to the 1800s. Once when workmen from the nearby sandpit were allowed to use the privy, one man went missing for a long time. When his workmates came to see what was keeping him, they were both amazed and amused to find him in the privy, deeply engrossed in reading *The Lady's Companion* magazines.

When Peggy was small and the nights were getting dark, she was afraid to visit the House of Lords on her own because she believed the foxes would get her. She does not know where this fear came from, but she still remembers that feeling of dread.

Peggy's brother, John, recalls one occasion when a pheasant straying from the neighbouring estate found its way via the

Rear view of the privy at Besthorpe, showing the ashpit.

ashpit into granny's privy, but was unable to get out again. When I innocently asked him what eventually happened to the bird, he simply smiled and said it tasted absolutely fine with bread sauce and all the trimmings!

Mrs Doris Corrie of Newark tells me that she married her first husband in 1952. As he was a German ex-POW, he was only allowed to do farmwork, so they worked on an estate farm belonging to a stately home, and lived in a tied cottage with an outside privy. Next to the privy they had an outdoor washhouse with a copper-sink, a dolly-tub and a mangle.

'It was a bind every Monday to empty the privy,' Doris says, adding that she chose Monday because it was washing day and there was plenty of hot water. On Sunday night she and her husband would dig a big hole in the orchard. The next day when her husband was at work and the children had gone to school, Doris would carry the privy bucket and empty it in the hole. She would fetch boiling water from the copper, rinse the bucket with it, then empty that water into the hole. Next she used to scrub the privy seat and floor with more boiling water. 'I had the cleanest toilet in the whole village,' she recalls with pride. By the time she had finished scrubbing out the privy, the effluence in the hole had sunk in, and she was able to fill it with soil.

Despite these unsophisticated arrangements, Doris says that people then were very content with their lives because everybody was in the same boat. She believes that nowadays. although people have more of life's luxuries, they want even more and are not as happy as in former times.

Mrs F. J. Klingbed of Syerston says that when she first moved to a farm in that village, she had an outside loo that was cosy and warm because it backed onto the kitchen fire. It was so warm that her stepfather used it to force rhubarb and even kept a working incubator in there. Her next door neighbour had a privy – memorably described by Mrs Klingbed as a 'Drop-It-And-Run' – down his yard. Using it one day in a hurry, she saw that it had a beautifully painted text hanging on the door, which read 'THOU, GOD, SEEST ME'. 'Being prudishly brought up,' she says, 'I didn't think He should!'

Another house Mrs Klingbed lived in had a little brick privy up the garden, which the family christened The Laurels. It had a beautiful view if the door was left open.

When she lived in Winkburn, there were four little buildings in the orchard. They were known as the kennels, but one of them housed the privy. This was for the use of the farmworkers, as the family had an indoor WC. This arrangement was fine until a bantam hen took up residence, laid her eggs and refused to move out.

The family then moved to a farm in Flintham; here the Drop-It-And-Run privy was in the yard. The walls of the privy were adorned with out of date calendars. It had a two-handled bucket underneath. The two German POWs had to be bribed with a Manikin cigar each to take the full bucket down to the farm muckyard. On one occasion they goose-stepped across the yard, but the handle came off the bucket. The bucket fell onto the stone causeway, splashing both men with the contents. Although what they said was in German, the gist of it was plain enough.

Later, a 25-gallon tank was installed underneath the privy. Grandpa gave the seat a sharp kick every time he went, saying he didn't want any rats to abbreviate him! He used to take a sheet of paper to the privy with him as well as a book. Having usefully occupied his time translating Horace or Virgil, he would then 'sacrifice the paper to Cloaca Maxima'. This phrase, first used by Lord Chesterfield in a letter to his son,

A privy at Saundby, in a yard that has not changed in appearance for 200 years.

refers to Cloaca, the Roman goddess of sewage, and to the Cloaca Maxima, the main drainage system of Rome.

When Mrs Klingbed returned to the farm at Syerston, the little fireback loo was rather dilapidated. While she was installed in there one day, her husband, waiting to follow her, leaned on the outside wall and commented. 'This lot'll have to come down.' He leaned a little harder and the wall **did** come down, bringing most of the roof with it. 'Luckily, this didn't include the part of the roof under which I was sitting,' says Mrs Klingbed. Being a handy and resourceful chap – as well as an over-enthusiastic demolition man – her husband knocked down the rest of the loo and built an extension to the house.

The house now has a proper indoor WC, kept warm by the hot water pipes and the flue from the Rayburn. They have no problems with poultry now, although the cat and her kittens do still like to claim squatters' rights.

John Robbins remembers his mother going to stay with her brother at Bunny. Here the privy was the bucket type that used to be collected by nightsoil men, who would remove it via a small door at the back. One day, as she sat on the privy, she had the unnerving experience of having the men removing the bucket from beneath her!

John also told me of the spinster lady who used to grumble constantly to her coalman that the coal he delivered was of poor quality, the lumps being too small to make a decent fire. After years of putting up with her complaints, the coalman eventually got even. In his yard, he found a slab of coal that weighed about a hundredweight, and decided that this lump ought to be big enough for his awkward customer. He took it to her house but instead of leaving it in the coalhouse he left it lying across the seat of her privy. John doesn't know how the lady solved her immediate needs until she could get the slab of coal removed, but he comments that she never grumbled about the size of her coal again.

Brian Curtis remembers growing up in the 1940s in the Mansfield Road area of Worksop. The house had a lean-to privy attached, which was served by an ashpit. The household ash was added to the privy waste, soaking up the wetness. Brian thinks that the pit was about a foot in depth, and says that the council sent men to dig it out every six months. The house is now a listed building, though its privy and ashpit have long gone.

Brian also remembers the row of privies at Oats Timber Yard

in Worksop. The waste from these was borne away by a channel of water that ran underneath. It was a common practice for some 'likely lad' to set fire to a crumpled newspaper and send it floating down the channel, causing cries of anguish to be heard from each occupied privy, as the burning paper passed beneath each sitting workman.

A similar story – though potentially even more dangerous – was told to me by Robin Fletcher of Saundby, near Retford, and harks back to when Mr Fletcher served with the colonial police force in Cyprus. Apparently the latrines serving the officers' mess of the Grenadier Guards in Nicosia consisted of a multi-holed seat over a long trench. As it was a latrine for officers, each hole was shielded from its neighbour by a sacking screen, to afford the occupants some privacy. After one social function, a junior officer was frustrated to find that every section in the latrine was occupied. In desperation, he went away, then returned with a can of petrol. He sloshed the petrol into the trench, lit a newspaper and tossed it in. The fire down below caused an immediate evacuation of the latrines, leaving it free – after a short cooling-off period – for the man's own use. There were several red faces (?) the next day, and when the culprit was identified, he spent the next few months on guard duty.

Robin Fletcher also told me about two police houses in south-west Nottinghamshire. He thinks that the precise village had better remain anonymous for reasons that will become clear. Each police house had a bucket privy and the two police constables were supposed to bury the contents each week. However, this was too much of a chore, so at midnight every Saturday, the two men would creep out, each with a full bucket in hand. They would wait until there was no traffic, then march out onto the main A1 road. One man standing on either side of the central white line, they would ceremoniously up-end the two buckets, tipping the contents onto the carriageway. By the time anyone was up and about on the Sunday morning, the traffic had spread the nightsoil so thinly for ten miles north and ten miles south of the original spot that no-one could tell what it was and where it came from. And all to save the trouble of digging a hole!

Robin also had a story from his own corner of north-west Notts. The local nightsoil man had been to a wedding and got himself thoroughly drunk. He was so inebriated that he decided it would be great fun to race his horse and nightsoil cart up and down the main street. Unfortunately the cart was fully loaded, and eventually it overturned, leaving its smelly contents all over the street. The Parish Council immediately dismissed the man from his job. However, the next few days were extremely hot and the street of the village where the spillage had occurred became very pungent. No-one was willing to take on the task of shovelling the offending material away, and the parish council-lors reluctantly reinstated the nightsoil man, on the strict condition his first task would be to remove the pile of nightsoil from the village.

George Webdill, the parish clerk of Cotham, told me a story about a Nottinghamshire village on the A1. Apparently, the 80-year-old resident of a picturesque old cottage in the village had finally decided to sell up and go to live with his daughter. When he put the cottage on the market, the estate agent he approached was delighted with the property and advertised it nationally. This led to a London lady, who liked the idea of moving to the country, travelling up to the East Midlands to look at the cottage. It lived up to her every expectation until she asked to use the lavatory. The old gentleman directed her to the bottom of the garden, where she found a ramshackle old

The entrance to this privy at Sturton-le-Steeple is well camouflaged.

building with no door. Inside, the fittings consisted of a plank with a round hole in it, suspended over a bucket. The lady's need was so great that she used the privy, her main concern being the fact that she could hear the A1 traffic below, the sound travelling in through the open doorway. Returning to the cottage, the lady told the old man that, given time, she might get used to the privy but that she thought it odd – foolish even – that it had no door. Surely it would be much more sensible to have a privy with a door on. 'Well, my dear,' he responded solemnly, 'it's been without a door for the eighty years I've lived here and I've never had a bucket stolen yet!'

[4]

THE TWELVE O'CLOCK 'OSSES

Many people believe that the days of the nightsoil men are over, and that the practice of using a bucket privy died out in the 1950s or possibly the 1960s. Wrong! There are still people today who go to the privy in the old-fashioned way, and who need the contents of their privy bucket collected every week. When I contacted Stewart Squires of Newark & Sherwood District Council, he informed me that BIFFA Environmental, the waste disposal company, had a council contract to collect privy waste from properties in the Newark/Southwell area. On his advice, I rang Roland Taylor, manager of the BIFFA depot at Southwell, and he confirmed that every Wednesday morning his men collected waste from privy buckets from seven houses locally. He 'made my day' by saying that I could accompany them, and take photographs of them about their task.

So, on the morning of Wednesday 8th July 1998, I set out to follow Bill Rice and Paul Leivers, the BIFFA crew, as they became the nightsoil collectors for the morning. Bill has been doing this job regularly for several years, but he has various assistants. Of course, the horse and cart of the old nightsoil men has long since disappeared, being replaced by a smart white tanker known as a Jetter-Vactor.

We trundled through rural East Nottinghamshire, through villages with evocative names like Kirklington, Maplebeck, Knapthorpe, Egmanton, Sutton-on-Trent, Barnby-in-the-Willows and – appropriately enough – Weecar. As we made the first couple of calls, it became obvious that Bill and Paul had got the task of bucket emptying off to a fine art. Bill drove the wagon; when they stopped at a house, Paul would go off to

40

The Biffa Jetter-Vactor – the modern nightsoil cart.

fetch the full bucket while Bill got the hose ready. The hose emptied the bucket in a matter of seconds, Paul swilled the bucket with disinfectant and returned it to the privy.

Some of the calls were at isolated farms and cottages, up narrow tracks that were only just wide enough for the tanker to pass, and one was at a rural scrapyard. Another was a smallholding nicknamed 'The Clampets', where hens, dogs, cats, horses and cows all live side by side, and I noticed a large dead rat at the side of the road. Other cottages we called on however, were in neat, attractive villages where all the neighbouring properties were connected to a septic tank or even to the main sewer. For one reason or another the owners of the houses we visited had chosen to remain faithful to the good old privy. The numbers involved are small though, and getting even smaller. 'There used to be nine calls,' Bill Rice told me, 'but we're down to seven now.'

Paul Leivers fetches the full bucket.

Bill Rice uses the hose to empty the bucket.

Paul returns the now empty bucket.

One call that slightly puzzled me was at a property where we slowed down, Bill staring at the gate before stopping. It appeared that the old gentleman who lived there had informed the crew, 'My bucket doesn't need emptying *every* Wednesday, because I'm an old man and I'm not that productive! If I want you to call, I'll attach a yellow clothes peg to my gate.' That was why we'd slowed down. Bill had been looking out for the yellow peg. It was there, so we stopped and Paul fetched out the bucket.

When the collecting had been completed, Bill drove over to Edwinstowe sewage works and the contents of the Jetter-Vactor were discharged into a channel to join the waste that had arrived via the more usual method of the main sewage pipe.

Bill commented that some of his colleagues laugh about his Wednesday morning run and say that they wouldn't do it at any price. 'But that's just daft,' is his reply. 'There's far worse jobs than this. Besides, somebody's got to do it, haven't they? Mind you,' he added with a grin, 'it's a bit different when the Jetter-Vactor vehicle isn't available and we have to go back to collecting with an ordinary van, pouring the waste from the buckets into a large dustbin with a lid tied on!'

Bill Rice is, of course, the present day equivalent of a long line of nightsoil collectors. In the Middle Ages they were known as gongfermors. The word 'gong' meant a privy and 'fermor' came from 'fey' meaning to cleanse. The occupation was very highly rated. In 1281, thirteen gongfermors were paid 7d each per night for raking out the cesspit at Newgate gaol, making them the best paid manual workers of their time. And they were allowed to supplement their income by selling on the waste to farmers to use as fertiliser. The job had its hazards; in 1326 a gongfermor named Richard the Raker fell through rotten flooring to drown in the nightsoil below. On the other hand, at the time of the plague, it was widely believed that the gongfermors were immune from catching that disease.

Gongfermors, or nightsoil men, have enjoyed a number of different nicknames over the years. Mrs Doleman of Annesley Woodhouse has lived in the same terraced street in Fox Street all her life. The houses, built in 1908, were among the first in that area to be built with flushing water supplied to the outside WCs. These loos were not fitted with lifting seats, but had a board – kept well-scrubbed, she recalls – with a hole in, over the lavatory bowl. There were only five houses with WCs, and these were attached to the wall of the house, whereas the older houses on the opposite side of the road had privies situated at the bottom of their gardens. The privies had buckets that had to be emptied by the nightsoil man, George Judson, who always called late on a Monday night. Mrs Doleman remembers lying in bed, listening to the horse and cart coming for the nightsoil, and being told by her mother, 'That's the twelve o'clock horses!' George Judson must have enjoyed calling at the houses in Fox Street because one of the neighbours always left him half a pint of beer to drink as he worked.

The twelve o'clock horses – or, as it is usually pronounced in Nottinghamshire, 'the twelve o'clock 'osses' – is one name for the nightsoil men with their cart. In other villages, where they must have called earlier, it's 'the ten o'clock 'osses'. Other names I have come across are the Dilly Men, the Lavender Men, the Midden Men and even the Honey Dumpers! Within the city of Nottingham, the Sanitary Men and the Corporation Men were common titles.

Sylvia Parker of Nottingham phoned to sing me a song about the nightsoil men, which her mother used to sing when she was a girl. It goes:

> The Sanitary Men
> Turn out at ten
> There ain't no men any bolder.

Out all night
In the pale moonlight
With their muck tubs on their shoulder.

Sylvia told me that her mother, who grew up in the Meadows area of Nottingham, was very proud of her maiden name, Miriam Ann Saltinstall. Sylia believes that the ancient name Saltinstall has now died out because all the children who inherited it were girls, who gave it up on marriage.

Duncan J. Walters of Mansfield sent me another version of this rhyme, saying that local children used to chant it whenever the nightsoil men were about. His version was:

The Corporation men
They turn out at ten
With their muck-tubs on their shoulder.
With knife and fork
To taste all sorts
And a stick to turn it over!

Duncan also passed on to me a story told to him by his father, William Benjamin Walters. Benjamin was one of six children raised in a terraced house in Newcastle Street, Huthwaite. During the winter of 1928–29, the well-trodden snow had hardened to a highly polished sheet of glass. At around ten o'clock, the familiar rumblings of the horse-drawn nightsoil cart were heard as it trundled across the cobbles on its approach to the wide alleyway at the end of the row. As it turned into the area between the houses and the outside privies (known locally as 'dry-pan lavs'), the cart began to slide across the ice. The nightsoil men – Bob and 'Kneely' Wright – panicked, and one of them pulled the lever attached to the mechanism which released the tumbrel. This upturned, emptying its contents all over the

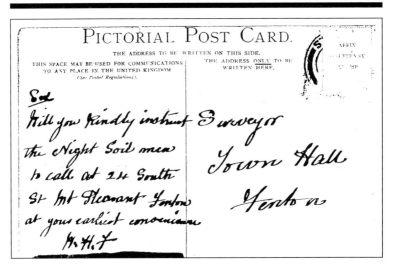

PICTORIAL POST CARD.

THE ADDRESS TO BE WRITTEN ON THIS SIDE.

THIS SPACE MAY BE USED FOR COMMUNICATIONS TO ANY PLACE IN THE UNITED KINGDOM *(See Postal Regulations).*

THE ADDRESS ONLY TO BE WRITTEN HERE.

AFFIX PENNY STAMP

Sir

Will you kindly instruct Surveyor the Night Soil men to call at 24 South St Mt Pleasant Fenton at your earliest convenience

M. H. F

Town Hall

Fenton

Postcard from Fenton, near Newark, once received by a Nottingham council – I love that 'at your earliest convenience'!

ground. It took several days and many gallons of disinfectant to clean up the mess. Even then, throughout the summer of 1929, whenever the backyards were warmed by the sun, there was still an odd disagreeable odour hanging around that end of the street.

All the nightsoil men had their own techniques. Mrs Sheila Henson of West Bridgford, who rang Radio Nottingham when I was talking about my researches (see chapter 10), said that the nightsoil men that she remembers in the 1940s brought out two buckets at a time, using a yoke across their shoulders, like the pictures of milkmaids in story books.

Kathleen Hordle of Farndon tells me that she feels that her family was very lucky as they didn't have to share a privy. However, she still remembers her childhood fear of going down the

Mr Wilson, the midden man at Farndon, with his horse Hyperion outside Farndon Chapel in 1944. (Photo taken by Kathleen Hordle's late sister, Lilian Toon)

garden at night and insisting that her mother accompanied her.

The nightsoil man – or 'midden man' as he was known in Farndon – was Mr Wilson, and he collected the nightsoil at two o'clock in the morning. Kathleen didn't like the sound of his cart coming so she would hide her head under the bedcovers. Mr Wilson collected the normal household rubbish by day and took it to a deep pit in Chapel Lane, surrounded by a fence. She is sure that there wasn't as much waste to dispose of in those days. Kathleen's father belonged to Farndon Pig Club, whose members used to keep one or two pigs to help with the meat rationing, so any food scraps were fed to the chickens or to the two pigs. Newspapers were cut up for use in the privy, or made into 'paper sticks' for lighting the fire.

In the early days, the nightsoil man lived in a caravan in a field next to the chapel. His horse was kept in the field, which

Bill Rice checks out a privy still in everyday use.

had a large walnut tree in it. As in the days of the gongfermors, nightsoil and refuse collecting must have been a well-paid occupation, because Mr Wilson was later to move from his humble caravan into a house 'built in the Italian style' on the old Fosse Way (A46), which was the former home of the local quarry owners.

At the bottom of Herbert Lewin's garden in Southwell lived Bill, who had the contract for collecting nightsoil from all of Southwell's privies. He would start his round at 10 pm and finish at 8 o'clock the next morning. Together with his helper, Scotty, Bill would drive round to each privy, and empty the contents of the buckets into his horse-drawn cart, known locally as the dilly cart. As they trotted along between calls, Scotty would sit on the back of the cart eating his snap. One morning in 1929, as Bill's fully laden dilly cart was on a road that skirted a wood, a pheasant flew out under the horse's legs. The horse shied, causing Scotty to fall backwards into the cartful of dung. Bill made him walk home that morning. Poor Scotty ended up standing in a stone trough with Bill pumping gallons of water over him. 'Keep on pumping,' Scotty kept yelling, 'I still stink!' The trough was situated by the Maythorne Silk Mill, and all the mill girls on their way to work were helpless with laughter at Scotty's expense. People made their own entertainment in those days!

[5]

NEWSPAPER, SPONGES
AND CORNCOBS

Many Nottinghamshire people who wrote to me related that, when they were children, it was their weekly task to cut the family newspaper into squares, make a hole in one corner and thread string through it. The newspaper squares were hung from a nail in the privy. They were there for wiping purposes, of course, though a secondary use was to read while sitting there. The snag with this was that the end of the story was always missing, having been used by a previous visitor. Another problem with using newspaper for wiping can be imagined by anyone who has ever noticed how just reading the newspaper results in inky hands from the newsprint.

Newspaper was not the only material to be used for the purpose, however. Excavations from the pits beneath medieval monasteries suggest that monks often used bits of rag from old habits. Aristocrats preferred to use strips of silk, and it is well recorded that in the 18th century, kings and queens would use goose feathers, often still attached to the dead bird. I bet that some poor servant then had the job of plucking the goose before despatching it to the royal kitchens!

In rural parts of the U.S.A., it was usual to find a box of corn-cobs in the privy, as these were the preferred form of wiping instrument. In ancient Rome, men used a 'mempira'. This was a piece of sea sponge, fastened in the end of something resembling a hockey stick, making it an ideal shape for reaching over the shoulder to the required area. In some communal latrines, there was a gulley of flowing water in which the mempirae were kept. After use, the instrument would be returned to the water so

52

Newspaper squares doubled as reading matter . . .

that it would be washed clean before its next use. There is a story of a Roman prisoner sentenced to death by stoning, avoiding that particularly unpleasant form of capital punishment by asking to use the latrine. There he removed the sponge from the stick and swallowed it, choking himself to death.

The earliest man probably used the handiest object for wiping himself – literally. He would use his hand. In certain cultures there developed a tradition of using the left hand for this purpose, reserving the right hand for eating, shaking hands and so on. Elsewhere, grass and leaves were considered better materials, and even twigs and pebbles! Modern man has reason to be grateful for toilet paper. Even there, some types are preferable to others. One gentleman insisted that hard shiny paper was no use at all, because it 'removes nothing, simply rearranges'.

Perhaps the days of newspaper squares were not too bad after all. If you were a specially favoured visitor, you might be really indulged. Two ladies told me that, although their own family had to use newspaper in the privy, their mother always saved the wrappers from oranges for important visitors – 'like the vicar' – to use.

[6]

THE VILLAGE SCENE:
PRIVIES IN KEYWORTH

Keyworth is a large village in the south of the county, and it has a flourishing local history society. Bob Hammond is an active member, and, after hearing of my interest in local privies, he undertook some researches of his own which he has kindly allowed me to use.

New Row used to run back from Main Street until it was demolished in the 1930s. It consisted of eleven cottages, which had the use of three two-holer privies, despite the fact that in 1891 there were 54 people living there. Even in the 1920s, one cottage housed a family of eight. In Bob's words, 'There must have been a good deal of uncomfortable waiting one's turn, especially during the rush hour.' The privies would all have had their newspaper squares hanging from a nail, and no doubt their fair share of large spiders and mice. Several people have told me how their dread of spiders can be traced back to the days of using the privies.

The privies were often shared between several households, and a rota would be required to organise whose turn it was to scrub the seats. Where this was not done properly, it could lead to neighbourhood disputes. My own local paper runs a series of features on what was being reported 100 years ago. One item – not from Keyworth – referred to a court case from August 1898, where a young miner stopped his neighbour's wife from using the shared privy, on the grounds that 'those who cleaned the privy should be the only ones using it, and as she hadn't taken her turn at cleaning she should take her business elsewhere!' Because the young man had physically seized the woman to prevent her from

55

entering the privy, he was found guilty of assault and given the option of a 24-shilling fine or seven days in prison.

It was also important to check that there were enough squares of newspaper hanging in the privy. To run out of paper – and not to notice until it was too late – was one of life's little cruelties. The privies were of course unheated, making a winter visit acutely chilly. They were unlit, too. During the daytime, visitors would have the benefit of light coming through gaps over and under the doors, but a visit during the hours of darkness would mean carrying a candle in a jam jar. No wonder that many people preferred the use of an indoor chamber pot at night!

The word privy means a private place, but the fact that several households shared these two-holer privies meant that there was very little privacy. Sociable types would sometimes sit happily side by side, but shy and sensitive individuals would have to keep a lookout from the house window until the privy was unoccupied, then make a dash for it. They would need to make haste because the doors had no locks, and another customer could turn up at any moment. May Stephenson's family moved into New Row when she was 14, and she recalls one incident when she opened the privy door to find a lady already sitting there. Although she was invited to come in and sit alongside the occupant, May fled in embarrassment. Despite this unpromising start, this meeting was the start of a good friendship and the two ladies were later to become sisters-in-law. May also remembers an occasion when a chimney sweep had to be called out to reach a sixpence that someone had dropped in the privy, and which had landed on a ledge just above the ashpit.

The cottages on Nottingham Road – unlike those on New Row – did have bolts on their privy doors. However, they were attached to the **outside** and were there only for preventing the doors from blowing to and fro when it was windy. Sybil Bouts recalls playing foxes and hounds – a variation of hide-and-seek

56

The three-seater privy when it was *in situ* at Shaw's Farm, Main Street, Keyworth. (Photo courtesy of Michael Meade)

– and she and a friend hid in one of the privies. They kept very quiet until one of the householders noticed that the door was ajar and bolted it from the outside. The two girls had to shout and scream until they were set free.

Originally, the privy waste fell into an ashpit, which was emptied every few months. The waste, mixed with ash and cinders, was dug out and piled in a heap to await collection. Margaret Sharpe remembers that sometimes the collector could be several days late, causing some unpleasantness for the residents.

When buckets under the privies replaced the old ashpits, the nightsoil had to be collected and taken away more frequently. Many older residents can remember the nightsoil man being Bob Smith of Lodge Farm on Wysall Lane. He came round

Adam Laugesen inspects the privy seat from Shaw's Farm, rescued by Keyworth Local History Society.

with a horse and cart and took the waste back to his farm for use as fertiliser. As he loaded the full buckets onto his cart, there would have been the occasional spillage, but although the smell must have been clinging and noticeable, Bob was always served without adverse comment when he called at the village chip shop for his lunch.

Bob Smith collected by day, but earlier nightsoil men would have done their collecting at night. A byelaw passed by Keyworth Parish Council in 1898 ordered that nightsoil was not to lie in the street after 9 am in winter or 8 am in summer. Bob Hammond deduces from this that there may have been complaints that the nightsoil man was not completing his collecting during the night, and the Parish Council was encouraging him to do so.

Shaw's Farm on Main Street had a large household because of the number of farm labourers and domestic servants who lived in. It is not surprising, therefore, that the privy here was a three-holer above an ashpit. Although the farm is no longer there – the farmhouse is now 36 Main Street – the outhouses were renovated only recently. Before the old privy was removed, Michael Meade, another member of Keyworth Local History Society, photographed it *in situ* (*see page 57*). The wooden three-seater board, complete with hinged lids, was rescued and is temporarily housed in Bob Hammond's garage. It is hoped to display it in a local museum one day.

Mains water arrived in Keyworth in the late 1920s but not all properties were connected to it immediately. Because of this, plus the lack of mains drainage, many households continued to use bucket closets for years to come and certainly one bungalow in Villa Road was using one until 1958. The village of Plumtree is about a mile north of Keyworth. When a farmhouse in the centre of the village was sold in 1975, the sale brochure mentioned that its one and only lavatory was an ashpit privy.

[7]

THE CITY SCENE: NOTTINGHAM

Of course, the removal of nightsoil and other refuse was a major undertaking in the city of Nottingham. Originally, it was allowed to stand around within the city until it rotted and acquired a value as fertiliser, when it could be sold and carted away by the 'muck majors', as they were known locally. Although a small amount was taken by cart directly into the fields just outside the city, most of the carts transported the nightsoil to a wharf on the Tinkers Leen section of the Nottingham Canal, where barges could take it out to the surrounding countryside via the Grantham Canal. Unfortunately, the nightsoil would leak into the canal itself. As the canal wharf was in a densely populated area, there were many complaints about the smell coming from the canal, particularly during the summer months.

Before 1867, the collecting of nightsoil was undertaken by private contractors. However, their carts were not 'leak-proof' and left unpleasant reminders of their work in the streets. Faced with this, plus the fact that the ashpits were not being thoroughly emptied, the Nottingham City Council invested £2,000 in providing the service themselves. They bought twenty-five carts and five wide canal barges, and constructed a platform at the edge of the canal so that the carts could be backed right up to the barges, and the nightsoil shot directly into the waiting boat. A water supply was provided, so that the carts could be washed after each visit to the wharf. The collecting was done during the night, and the barges would depart each morning.

The Council also decided to collect general household rubbish separately so that the nightsoil they were selling for use on the land would be of good quality, with no pieces of extraneous rubbish. Prior to this, the nightsoil would contain pieces of broken pottery, clay pipes and so on, which was not appreciated by the farmers spreading the manure on their fields.

By 1873, the new system seemed to be working well. The Sanitary Committee employed 48 men, working in gangs of four, to collect the contents of the city's ashpits and bucket privies. Each gang of four had two carts and one horse, and they worked continuously from 10 pm until 7 am. At the canal wharf, three men known as trimmers, working under a superintendent, picked out any pieces of debris (such as broken pottery) from the nightsoil.

Despite the good service given by this system of moving nightsoil by canal, a number of factors led the Council to move towards the use of railway transport. The Great Northern Railway Company built a 'manuring siding' in Nottingham, and more and more of the nightsoil was moved by rail. By 1863, the Sanitary Committee owned seventy-three railway wagons compared with eight barges, and it was decided to purchase even more wagons. Although the vast majority of nightsoil was being transported via the railways, evidence from discoveries made on farmland along the banks of the canals suggests that some nightsoil continued to be taken via the canal system as late as the 1920s.

[8]

THOSE WERE THE DAYS

Suzanne Vaulkhard now lives in Kinoulton, but her tale of a childhood memory comes from Woodthorpe. At the bottom of Woodthorpe Drive was a lovely old cottage which may once have been a gatehouse to the Park. The lady who lived there was Mrs Roberts, a friend of Suzanne's mother. Mrs Roberts was quite a character and one of Suzanne's earliest memories is being taught by her how to ride on a pig!

The privy at Mrs Roberts' cottage was across a yard. When anyone went to use it they had to carry a broom to fend off the aggressive cockerel which had an extremely possessive attitude to its territory. Suzanne recalled that to gain the sanctuary of the privy, she had to run as fast as she could, dodging the attentions of this fierce fowl. Once she was in the privy, she then had to sit and worry about the return trip. As a small girl, she spent far more time than she should inside that privy, simply because she couldn't fathom out how she was going to get back to the house in one piece!

———————————

Miss J. E. Sparrow tells me that in 1932, her father was living with his parents in an ancient cottage in Chapel Street, Beeston. The privies belonging to these cottages were some distance behind the dwellings. A lad called Tony Lee lived in another of the cottages and, although Tony was at 12 the oldest of the four local boys, he was terrified of the dark. The other boys used to tease him, and delighted in spreading a story that Tony had been spanked by his grandmother for using her washtub rather than make a night-time visit across to the privy.

There seems no doubt who owns this two-seater privy at Inkersall Farm, Bilsthorpe.

John Sidebotham outside his two-seater privy at White Borough Farm, Huthwaite.

To make things worse, Miss Sparrow's father had told Tony a completely fictitious tale about the area being haunted by the ghost of a headless woman who walked about on dark and foggy nights.

The boys, full of devilment, decided to play a rather cruel trick on their nervous friend. They obtained a dressmakers' dummy from the local junkyard, and sawed off the stand to leave just the torso. One of the boys daubed some blood-red paint around its neck, finally draping a sheet around the whole. After dark, the conspirators quietly deposited their creation on the Lee family privy, and settled down to wait for Tony to pay his bedtime visit.

However, it wasn't young Tony who made the journey across the yard from the cottage to the privy, but his 80-year-old granny. The gang of watching boys found their emotions change from mischievous glee to apprehensive panic as they saw the frail old lady in her carpet slippers shuffle past with a flickering candle in her hand. They watched helplessly as she opened the door and went in. Seconds later, the silent darkness of Chapel Street was shattered by hysterical screaming as the old lady encountered the headless 'ghost', then collapsed with shock.

At lightning speed the three boys shot to their respective homes and put themselves to bed. Poor old Granny Lee was carried indoors and the police were summoned. The next day, all the boys in Chapel Street received a visitation from the local bobby, and several were given a clip round the ear by their mothers just in case they'd been involved. However, no one admitted anything. Fortunately the old lady survived the shock, although Miss Sparrow doubts that she ever appreciated the funny side of the prank.

Chapel Street and its privies are long gone, replaced by a multi-storey car-park, but Miss Sparrow says that her father still sports a schoolboy smirk on his face whenever he walks past.

As a child, Sylvia Brotherhood of Sherwood lived in a three-storey house with two very small rooms downstairs and four up. The house had no bathroom or inside loo, but there was a lavatory next to the coalhouse in the back yard. She remembers her father rigging up an electric light in the outside privy which ran off a switch in the kitchen. The light was for the use of the person in the loo of course, but it had a secondary use. When the privy was occupied, anyone waiting to go would flick the switch on and off to encourage the occupant to get a move one. Sylvia's father, a collier, used to always take a book in with him, but it wasn't advisable to give him the hurry-up signal with the light switch, because he would 'go mad'.

Sylvia says that her most embarrassing moment occurred when she was eleven years old. She came running in from school one day, desperate to use the toilet. She burst in through the front door, raced across the kitchen, and out of the back door. She heard her mother shout something as she passed, but Sylvia's need was too pressing to stop and listen. She rushed down the three steps, entered the loo and sat down in relief. She then discovered that her mother had been trying to tell her that the wooden loo seat had just been painted with bright green gloss paint! Her mother came and peeled her off the seat, and Sylvia then spent a very traumatic hour standing on a chair, having lard rubbed into her bum and legs to get the green paint off. It wasn't very nice at the time, Sylvia says, but retelling the event has caused a lot of merriment over the years since.

Mrs Madge Wallhead now lives in Edwinstowe, in the heart of Sherwood Forest, but she grew up in the town of Warsop before going into service. She remembers her mother scrubbing the seat of the privy with boiling water from the boiler in the wash-house. Although the wash-house was shared with other families in the square where they lived, Madge's family – the Rileys – were very fortunate to have a privy all to themselves. 'We thought we were very posh,' she says, 'as the other families had to share one.'

Although the seat was kept scrubbed, Madge is sure that there was no lid to the privy and that it used to begin to smell when it was getting full. The nightsoil men used to come with their horse and cart to empty the privy at midnight.

Ralph Flintoff was a carpenter working on Nottinghamshire building sites for all his working life, and in the 1930s he was part of a team converting over 400 houses in the village of Brinsley from the old privies to the new WCs. The new flushing lavatories were to be much nearer to hand. Most of the villagers had been using the privy at the bottom of their gardens for many generations, but the new loos were installed in the coalhouses attached to the houses. Ralph told me that it was his job to put in the wooden supports to hold the water cisterns, but on one of his first installations, he was berated by the woman of the house. His hammering in the coalhouse had caused the pots and pans to fall off the wall of the kitchen the other side of the wall. Ralph was under the impression that the walls were 9 inches thick, but this proved incorrect; they were only half that thickness. He worked more gently on the rest of the conversions.

Ralph said that in many of the old privies, he noticed a stick about 30 inches in length, leaning against the wall. When he asked what it was for, he was told that the stick was used to poke down any paper that was floating on top of the pit, or to rearrange the pile of dung if it was beginning to assume a pyramid shape. 'It was essential to keep one end of the stick for poking down the privy,' he explained, 'and keep the clean end as a handle.' He is certain that this practice is the origin of the phrase 'to get the mucky end of the stick'.

Ralph Flintoff also told me that, whenever they were moving onto a new building site it was his task to get there before work began and to build a latrine for the men to use. He would dig a deep hole, then construct a supported beam over it for workmen to sit on. The addition of four walls and roof completed the building of this simple privy. 'I had to estimate how deep to dig the initial hole,' he told me. 'It was a bit of a disaster if the building work on the site lasted longer than the hole under the privy took to fill!'

Peter Stephens of Newark Civic Trust says that the most remarkable lavatory he ever encountered was the away supporters' area at Meadow Lane, home of Britain's oldest professional football club, Notts County. I will ignore the obvious question of what a Nottinghamshire resident was doing in the *away* enclosure. Peter says that the away fans used to dread being 'caught short' and having to use this antiquated contraption. The loo, which was probably Victorian, was flushed by means of a massive kick-down lever, fiendishly sited about a foot from the floor. Using it called for powerful calf muscles, and Peter likens the action to firing an old-fashioned Brough Superior motor cycle, except that the flush lever was considerably harder to make work.

Jenny Parker of East Drayton says she still remembers graduating from her childhood potty to the more grown-up outside two-seater privy. The privy nestled between the pigsty, complete with pig, and the very spidery woodshed. She traces her present intense fear of spiders to the same graduation. Jenny says that as well as using the traditional squares of newspaper in the privy, her mother used to make life a little easier for her by scrunching up old dressmaking patterns.

A two-seater privy at Sand Lane, Besthorpe, designed to seat an adult and child.

An event that she will never forget occurred one summer Saturday morning in the late 1950s. Jenny and her mother always took their summer holiday in Mablethorpe with her aunt and three cousins. On this day; the taxi had arrived and had been loaded with suitcases and buckets and spades. It was time for the children to make a final visit to the privy before beginning the journey from East Drayton to the seaside. Cousin William, who would have been about seven at the time, insisted that he was old enough to go on his own. However, on this occasion, the family became impatient when he seemed to be taking a long time over his visit. 'He's messing about in there again,' his mother commented, before going to hurry him up. What a sight met her eyes! She found that William had – for reasons known only to himself – decided to sit down to 'spend a penny', only to

This two seater privy at Huthwaite was for two adults.

fall backwards into the hole. Jenny comments that cousin William 'was not a pretty sight and was certainly not smelling of roses!' The family set off for their holiday much later that day, after Master William had been scrubbed down with a bar of carbolic soap. Just to compound his problems, William was extremely travel-sick on the way. 'It's a wonder we ever got anywhere with him,' Jenny comments.

June Smith, also of East Drayton, wrote to give me a story told to her by her neighbour, which he swears is true. A visitor to East Drayton went down the garden to use an old privy, and on his return to the house he said to the owner, 'My goodness, did you know that your closet was full of blowflies?'' The owner's laconic reply was, 'Well you should have waited and gone at dinner time

This unusual two-seater privy at Sturton-le-Steeple had an additional rectangular hole, probably for ash.

A privy – still in use – at Bathley.

because all the flies will be round this table then.'

June also relates an incident which occurred during the war. A farm in the village had two or three German prisoners-of-war working there, and the farmer's wife could not get on with one of them. She waited until he was sitting on the privy, opened the little ashpit door at the back, and pushed some burning newspaper under his bottom.

Dorothy Roberts of Worksop recalls several outside privies from her younger days, as she has lived in different villages. She particularly remembers one from her teenage years, because she papered it with pages of her comics, using the traditional flour-and-water paste. She says that everyone in her family used to enjoy reading the wallpaper as they sat in that privy. The skills she acquired then were certainly not wasted, as she has drawn on her earlier experience in wallpapering to do her own decorating ever since.

Lynne Morley of Balderton says that the luxury of modern-day soft toilet paper is the one thing that causes her to be grateful she is living in the present age. She adds that her ultimate nightmare is being in a toilet where the only material available is either old newspapers or something that feels like recycled sandpaper. She hates the idea of using old newspapers because she argues that if they leave print all over your hands when you read them, where would the headlines end up if you used them in the privy?

Lynne remembers many family tales about the privies of old Newark. In particular, her mum used to talk about visiting an aunt and uncle who lived on the banks of the Trent, close to a weir. Their privy was situated at the bottom of the garden, near the pigsty that was home to two porkers called Primrose and

Winston. Lynne believes that the cocktail of aromas from the privy and the pigsty must have been truly horrific. There was no heating in the privy, so in the bleak midwinter months haemorrhoids were a constant hazard. Unlike his neighbours, this uncle had no need of the services of the nightsoil men to empty his privy bucket. He had his own method. He would carefully take the full bucket to the garden fence that separated his property from the river, and throw the foul contents into the raging torrents of the weir. This simple solution to waste disposal seemed ideal to him, though Lynne thinks that people living downstream – not to mention all the anglers on the bank – may have had a different opinion. She says that when her great-uncle's cottage was eventually pulled down, it must have come as a great relief to the neighbours. The fact that in later years a sewage works was built on the site where the cottage once stood is somewhat ironic. In Lynne Morley's own words, 'The sanitary plant stands as a monument to a man who played his particular part in water pollution!' Lynne has drawn a cartoon of what used to happen when her mother was a young girl visiting the aunt and uncle by the Trent. (*see page 75*)

June Yeomans remembers visiting her Aunt Mary, who lived down Tolney Lane in Newark, in the 1940s. The outside privy there was what June refers to as 'one of those horrible smelly wooden contraptions'. 'You didn't spend very long in there, I can tell you,' she reminisces wryly. She also recalls privies in Albion Street, where her Granny Fincham lived. Her granny's privy had just one seat, but some of the houses in Albion Street had two-holer privies, which June found very strange.

June's father was a dustman by day, but on Friday nights he became the local nightsoil man, collecting and taking away the contents of the privy buckets. Very few men were willing to do

Cartoon, courtesy of Lynne Morley.

the job, but he did it because it was so well paid. June says that
on Friday nights people would keep their bedroom windows
firmly shut to keep out the terrible stench. Her father often used

75

to comment that if anyone spilled any of the contents on his clothes, he would 'reek to high heaven'.

An 82-year-old gentleman says that he used to live in Jubilee Cottages, Sutton-in-Ashfield. He recalls that in the 1930s, the nightsoil men used to take the privy waste to a tip in Columbia Avenue. However, one of the men used to divert the cart to empty some of the load onto his allotment, with the result that he grew the biggest and best vegetables in the town.

The same gentleman also remembers visiting a multi-seater privy in Baghdad, which had a very long drop. 'You could count to twenty before you heard the splash!' he reminisced with a chuckle.

Peter Shaw recalls his family moving to a council house in Hall Street, Mansfield, when he was eleven. This house had the luxury of possessing both an outside loo and an indoor one situated in the bathroom. This should have been a big improvement on their previous home, a terraced house with just an outside loo, but it didn't quite work that way. 'We had to carry on using the outside toilet,' Peter reminisces, 'because Mum didn't allow us to use the bathroom. She said that going to the toilet inside the house was unhygienic!'

Later, Peter's elder brother left home and went to live in Gladstone Street, Kirkby-in-Ashfield. Here the houses had to share an outside WC, as there were four toilets to eight houses. Peter says that when he visited his brother he noticed that the ancient loo had a very rusty cistern. His brother warned him not to pull the chain in case he brought the whole thing tumbling down. Instead he would have to take a bucket of water from the

A row of outside WCs like these in Edwinstowe was quite common.

house in order to flush it. This anecdote reminded Peter of a story he'd been told about an incident which had occurred during the war. As a man sat on his outside WC, the bombs fell, wreaking havoc all around him. Although several neighbouring houses took direct hits, and the loo he was in rattled and shook, the man escaped without any injury. Feeling lucky to have survived without a single scratch, he stood up and pulled the chain, causing the loosened cistern to crash down on his head!

[9]

GEORGINA AND THE BOMB

Mrs Georgina White tells me that in 1942 she was a 15-year-old girl working at a farm in Gringley-on-the-Hill as a live-in house-maid and dairymaid. Part of her duties was to deliver milk on her bicycle, milk cans on one handlebar and a lidded milk pail on the other. The cans – some half-pints and some pints – were left on customers' doorsteps, and at other houses she ladled milk from the pail into their own jugs.

Early one morning in May, Georgina woke up and looked out of the bathroom window. It was bright moonlight, but she rea-lised that she could also see flames. She woke the 'master', Mr Walker, telling him that she thought the nearby town of Gains-borough was on fire. Mr Walker looked out and said, 'It's not Gainsborough. They seem to be bombing Gringley!' Georgina thinks that the German pilot had mistaken the wet shiny road for the River Trent, and the covered farm machinery by the roadside for a factory. Between them, Mr Walker and Georgina managed to rouse a sedated Mrs Walker, and the three of them took shelter under the stairs. They had not been there long before there was a loud explosion very close to the house.

At daylight they discovered that a bomb had dropped on the farm's stockyard, known locally as the crewyard. Luckily, the cattle had been put out to grass the day before. The bomb had knocked out all the doors and windows, sending rubble every-where, and covering all the buildings with manure. The path to the privy was covered in rubble, and fallen telegraph wires blocked the way.

Young Georgina, desperate to go to the loo, asked Ray, the local Air Raid Warden if he could help her make her way there.

All's well that ends well – Georgina at 18. (Photo courtesy of Georgina White)

He agreed and accompanied her over the obstacles. When they got there, they found that, although the door had been blown off its hinges, the privy was still usable. Ray waited round the side of the privy while Georgina went in. As she sat there, she called out to him, 'Ray, stand further away. I can hear your watch ticking really loud.' Ray's hand came in through the open doorway and unceremoniously yanked the young girl off the privy, as he yelled, 'Run! I'm not wearing a watch!' What Georgina had heard was, in fact, the ticking of an unexploded timebomb lying at her feet.

Later, when she was questioned by the military authorities, they told her somewhat brusquely that she had probably set off the ticking mechanism herself when she entered the privy and she was very lucky not to have been blown to Hell! Georgina calmly told her interrogators that Hell wasn't quite ready for her yet. The two things that annoyed her most about the whole traumatic experience were (a) the embarrassment of being pulled off the privy, and (b) the fact that when she and the Air Raid Warden ran from the scene she lost her brand new slippers in the tangle of telegraph wires. She had saved up for those slippers, and had used up valuable clothing coupons!

Strangely, when the farm labourer arrived from the other side of the village later that day, he was amazed at the scene. He had heard nothing of it. Another fact that brought a smile to my face was that at that time Georgina's surname was Christmas. 'Yes,' she informed me, 'I went from being Miss Christmas to being Mrs White. Perhaps I ought to combine both names and call myself Mrs White-Christmas!'

[1 0]

PRIVY TALK

One of the best ways of reaching a wide number of people in a region is by way of local radio. On Thursday 27th August 1998, I appeared on Nick Brunger's afternoon show on BBC Radio Nottingham, talking about my researches into local privies and chatting with listeners who rang in during the piece.

After introducing me and talking about my project, Nick mentioned that he had recently interviewed some ladies who had been in the Land Army. One of them described how they had been billeted in a very grand house where the bathroom was so elaborate that they had to twist gargoyles to make the water flow into the bath; they had eventually found the lavatory by lifting the plush velvet seat of what appeared to be a throne. I reminded Nick that this kind of close stool within a throne was what King Louis XIV of France had sat on while receiving diplomats and foreign guests during the 17th century.

While we waited for our first caller, Nick told me of a privy he had once visited that hung over a stream, taking advantage of what he called 'organic plumbing'. We contemplated the reactions of downstream dwellers of what were regarded as clear water streams. When we got onto the topic of three and four-holer privies, Nick told me of a Roman multi-hole privy he'd visited on the island of Cyprus, where 20 men at a time could use the latrine – and hold a conversation.

The first listener to ring in was Tom from Tuxford, who recalled his days in the Navy. He had served in submarines, where the lavatories – or heads – depended on a series of linkage valves and levers to force the rubbish out into the sea. However, every now and then, someone would operate the wrong lever, or

An old privy – now used as a garden shed – in East Leake.

A beautiful view from a privy at Sturton-le-Steeple.

a valve would misfire. The occupant of the lavatory would hear a *whoomph* and the effluence would backfire into his face. This apparently led to a lot of laughter from everyone aboard except the recipient. Tom also had experience of multi-occupant latrines, including a six-holer in a dry-dock posting. He remembers one sailor setting fire to a newspaper and sending it down the gutter under the latrine, causing 'a lot of sun-tanned posteriors!'

Nick mentioned that he had seen a photograph of a privy that was built on wheels so that it could be moved to different parts of the garden whenever the ashpit beneath it was full. My comment was that it had been quite common for residents to sit in their privy with the door open, taking full advantage of the sunshine and views. An additional advantage of a privy on wheels might be that it would be possible to rotate it during the day to face the sun.

Our second caller, Fred from Bulwell, had a story from his schooldays in the 1930s. The bucket privies used to be emptied by the school caretaker by means of a swinging wooden door underneath, and the contents tipped into a field behind the school. At playtime, the boys delighted in collecting nettles and thistles, and pushing them into the backdoor of the girls' privies in such a way that the next user would find herself sitting on a very prickly seat. 'When we went back into class,' Fred chuckled, 'you could always tell who'd been to the privy because they'd be scratching themselves all afternoon'.

Katherine Mart of Bilborough rang to say that as a girl she used to live in the Narrow Marsh area of Nottingham. She remembers the days of the privy, and recalls her parents announcing the arrival of the nightsoil cart with the phrase, 'The ten o'clock hosses are coming!', which used to frighten her at the time. She also told a tale of when her husband was a young man out in Australia. His visit to the 'dunny' was once interrupted by a six foot long killer snake. He obviously survived and brought home a photo of the snake to prove his tale was true. Nick commented that, fortunately, killer snakes were not a problem in Nottinghamshire privies. 'The spiders grew pretty big, though,' was my own contribution.

Doug from Arnold rang in with a story about Nottingham Ice Stadium. He had a friend whose job involved directing the spotlights onto the performers in the various skating shows held there. The spotlight men had to work in the space above the false ceiling. On one occasion, during an ice pantomime, his friend was 'taken short' and had to make his way over to another part of the roof space where an empty oil drum had been provided for just such an emergency. Unfortunately, he slipped and his foot fell through the ceiling, showering the audience with dust and pieces of plaster. Appropriately enough, the singer below was belting out, 'Answer me, Lord above'.

Joan Hampton of Sherwood Rise, Nottingham described this salt-glazed lavatory pan – now used as a plant container – when she rang the Nick Brunger radio programme.

Nick and I then got onto the topic of phrases used to indicate going to the loo. One he recalled his great aunt saying was, 'Going to visit Mrs Murphy'. He thought that this might have originated from a maker of sanitary porcelain named Murphy, although it was not one I'd come across. I reminded him that the most common trade name found on lavatory pans and urinals was 'Armitage Shanks', and was able to tell him of the graffiti I'd once seen added under that name which read, 'Well, who is Armitage and what is shanking?'

My afternoon with Radio Nottingham was indeed a very well spent one, and added greatly to my researches into the county's privies.

[11]

LITERATURE AND LEGENDS

One of Nottinghamshire's most famous sons is Lord Byron, who inherited both his title and the family seat at Newstead Abbey in 1798, when he was ten years old, following the death of his great-uncle. He was a complex personality, combining aristocratic vices with commendable support for radical causes. He spoke up in Parliament on behalf of the poor, particularly the Nottinghamshire frame knitters, but also became notorious for his amorous liaisons throughout Europe. One of his less glorious moments was when he was barred from Long's Hotel in Bond Street, for deciding one cold wet night to defecate behind the curtains of the hall rather than face the trip to the outside privy situated in an uncovered yard! Given that this had been a common practice in former times, the hotel's disapproval might be seen as a sign of progress.

Byron's poetry is deservedly famous, but for some reason, his *Childe Harold* and *Don Juan* are far better known than the words he wrote on the subject of going to the privy. I will attempt to remedy this omission. With the twin evils of constipation and diarrhoea in mind, Byron addressed his poem to Cloacina, the Roman goddess of the privy.

> O Cloacina, Goddess of this place
> Look on thy supplicants with a smiling face.
> Soft yet cohesive let their offerings flow
> Neither too swift nor yet unduly slow.

One of the earliest literary references to privies occurs in the Old Testament, where Moses instructs his followers to use a place outside their camp. 'Thou shalt have a place also without the camp, wither thou shalt go forth abroad. And thou shalt have a paddle upon thy weapon; and it shall be, when thou wilt ease thyself abroad, thou shalt dig therewith, and shalt turn back and cover that which cometh from thee' (Deuteronomy XXIII *12–13*).

Reading these instructions from three thousand years ago, it strikes me that Moses was describing how to build a simple privy. Take that hole in the ground, add four walls and a roof, and the result would be recognisable as a Nottinghamshire privy of any time between the 15th and early 20th centuries! And how wise that advice to cover up 'that which cometh from thee'. A user of the local privy would throw in ashes or sand in exactly the same way.

One of my heroes is Sir John Harington, whose invention of the Mighty Ajax – England's first flushing loo – is described in chapter 1. Harington upset his 16th-century religious contemporaries by writing a poem in which he imagines a priest accidentally invoking the Devil by saying his prayers while sitting on the privy!

> A godly father sitting on a draught
> To do as need and nature hath us taught,
> Mumbled – as was his manner – certain prayers,
> And unto him the devil straight repairs,
> And boldly to revile him he begins
> Alleging that such prayers were deadly sins,
> And that he shewed he was devoid of grace
> To speak to God from so unmete a place.
>
> The reverend man, though at first dismayed,
> Yet strong in faith, to Satan thus he said:
> 'Thou damned spirit, wicked, false and lying,

Despairing thine own good, and ours envying,
Each take his due, and me thou canst not hurt,
To God my prayer I meant, to thee the dirt.
Pure prayer ascends to Him that high doth sit,
Down falls the filth, for friends of Hell more fit.

Another writer who wrote the great wit and humour on the subject of the privy was the late Rhys Davies. In his story, *The Contraption*, he describes how the elderly ladies living in some village almshouses take on the authorities who wish to impose a new indoor flushing toilet on them. The power struggle between the residents and Mrs Hope-Cary, a new powerful member of the committee running the almshouses, comes to a head when the ladies' spokeswoman, Sarah Crump, says that rather than use the new contraption, the ladies will go back to using the hedgerows and fields! *Her ladies*, Sarah Crump avows, *will never sit over water!* Fortunately, the almshouses residents win and are able to continue using the old outside privy for the rest of their days, while the new contraption is left unused to gather dust and cobwebs. Such a sweet victory! And it certainly echoes the views of a number of Nottinghamshire people who told me that their parents never really approved of the seemingly unhygienic modern idea of siting the toilet inside the house, even inside the bathroom. Surely the bottom of the garden was a more appropriate location.

Another power struggle on a similar subject occurs in the French novel *Clochemerle* by Gabriel Chevallier. When the village authorities of Clochemerle decide to construct a men's urinal, it seems like a progressive move. However, the chosen site is opposite the church and the debate turns into a political dog-fight between the left-leaning council and the powerful Roman Catholic hierarchy. The book has some wonderfully humorous scenes and

89

witty comments. At one point, Chevallier has one of his charac-
ters talk of the twin pleasures of drinking wine without stint and
the subsequent delight of seeking relief to its utmost possibility,
without haste or hurry, in a fresh, well-ventilated place. Could
any civilised man disagree?

John Dryden, the 17th-century Poet Laureate, had in mind the
dangers late night revellers faced when walking home through
the streets of any city in England. He advised getting home
before dawn, as that was when householders would empty their
chamber pots from an upstairs window. Those householders
who were considerate would shout 'Gardy loo' as they did so,
but the warning cry was often too late for the passer-by beneath.
Dryden tells his readers that they should count themselves fortunate if the falling waste is simply in liquid form!

> As many fates attend thy steps to meet
> As there are waking windows in the street;
> Bless the good gods, and think thy chance is rare,
> To have a pisspot only for they share.

The book *The Specialist*, first published in England in 1930 and
still in print – and that must constitute some kind of record – is
the classic book on the subject of privies. It describes the work of
Lem Putt, a specialist in the building of privies in rural America,
quoting his down-to-earth advice on the subject. Much of this
advice holds true for Nottinghamshire privies too.

For example, Lem suggests that the privy be built near the
woodpile. That way, not only can the user bring back a couple
of logs every time he uses the privy, it also gives a legitimate
excuse for any lady too shy to want people to know where she is
going. She can approach the woodpile, then veer off to her real
destination if there is no-one about. Several Nottinghamshire

90

This one-seater privy at Barnby-in-the-Willows is still used everyday – note the inward opening door.

'Gardez-loo!' This Hogarth illustration of 1738 shows the dangers of walking carelessly beneath an open window.

ladies have related that some of their more reticent friends were always very glad that the dustbin was situated next to the privy. They could nip out to the bin carrying some refuse, then, if the coast was clear, they could go to use the privy. There was very little privacy for most people when they went to the privy. Mrs Klingbed of Syerston recalls an incident that occurred soon after her marriage. Her privy was situated in a coalshed. On one occasion while she was using it, the insurance man called, and she heard her neighbour's clarion voice shouting, 'She won't be long. I've just seen her going into the privy!'

Many people have confided to me that one of their greatest pleasures was to sit in their privy with the door wide open, enjoying the sunshine and the beautiful view of the Nottinghamshire landscape. This was possible because the privy faced away from the house, and because the privy door opened inwards. This reflects another piece of Lem Putt's advice: never make the door open outwards. With an inward-opening door, the occupant can sit in his privy with his foot by the open door. If he hears anyone approaching, he can simply kick the door shut. However, an outward-opening door would entail a panicky dash with shirt-tail flapping to close it.

The Specialist was written by Charles Sale, but it is one of life's delightful coincidences that it was illustrated by the appropriately named William Kermode!

An amusing legend is the apocryphal tale concerning Noah and his adventures aboard his Ark. With the best of intentions, Noah was hoarding all the dung produced by his crew – animal and human – so that he could use it to fertilise the land when the waters had receded. However, the amount produced over the forty days and the forty nights was so tremendous that it seemed the Ark would sink. At the request of his family, Noah reluctantly agreed to jettison his cargo of manure. It was thrown overboard, only to form a new island. Varying versions of this legend claim that the island concerned is either Crete, Cyprus or Malta.

I REMEMBER IT WELL

And finally . . . Local poet Malcolm Tudor has continued the
tradition of privy poetry with these nostalgic lines:

I remember the old privy at the bottom of the yard
With rough brick walls and slated roof; the door was creosote
    tarred.
And in that door there was a hole you'd poke your finger
    through
To lift the latch, to get inside and do what you must do.

The seat was made of timber that reached from wall to wall,
And in the middle, gaping, was a large repulsive hole.
For beneath it was a bucket that was emptied every week,
And coming up to Friday, the stronger grew the reek.

The walls inside were whitewashed; there was no electric light,
So you took a match and candle when you visited at night.
And the flame it used to flicker with the draught beneath the
    door,
While your shadow danced in unison upon the concrete floor.

We had no use for toilet rolls, soft tissues and the like,
But tore up last week's *Radio Times* and stuck it on a spike.
Then before we came to use it, we would crumple every sheet,
And with backsides stained with printers' ink, we'd beat a quick
    retreat.

Then in the height of Summer there came the hordes of flies,
And the catalyst of temperature caused the smells to rise.
So, if someone put the lid on the hole that's in the seat,
The next one in to lift it had two lungs full, rich and neat.

But Winter proved the hardest, for when you had to go,
You grabbed the nearest shovel for a pathway through the snow.
And the thermal shock you suffered, as you sat upon the seat,
Made you long for constipation to make you last a week.

Now we've got an inside toilet, and it's central heated too.
The walls are smooth and plastered and it's painted pastel blue.
We've electric lighting also, but it's not quite what we'd like,
For the *Radio Times* is missing – they forgot the blasted spike!

ACKNOWLEDGEMENTS

I would like to thank Radio Nottingham; the editors of all the local newspapers who allowed me to appeal for information from their readers; the conservation officers of Nottinghamshire's local authorities; Peter Hammond of West Bridgford who allowed me to plunder an article he wrote for *The Nottinghamshire Historian*; Bob Hammond (no relation) of Keyworth' Local History Society; Robert Cox of Nottingham Industrial Museum, and BIFFA Environmental (Southwell), who allowed me to go out with their Wednesday morning privy bucket emptying team!

I also acknowledge help and information given to me by: Mrs Mabel Barber, Robert P. L. Brackenbury, Mr and Mrs Robin Brackenbury, Mrs Peggy Bristow; Sylvia Brotherhood, Miss Bullock, Mrs Cheetham, David Cheetham, Doris Corrie, Brian Curtiss, Mrs Doleman, Mr Draycott, J. Duncan, Mr Fisher, Helen Flarry, Robin and Madge Fletcher, Ralph Flintoff, Marjorie Goodcliffe, The Rt Rev Patrick B Harris, Bishop of Southwell, and his staff, Shirley Horton, Kathleen Hordle, Wayne Jacks, Phil Jackson, Mrs E. Johnson, Mrs F. J. Klingbed, Paul Leivers, Barbara Legge, Herbert Lewin, Michael Meade, Ian Moat, Lynne Morley, David Otter, Paula Panayi, Jenny Parker, Sylvia Parker, Mr Pix, E. R. Radcliffe, Bill Rice, Cliff Ringer-Bond, John Robbins, Dorothy Roberts, Peter Shaw, John Sidebotham, June M. Smith, Miss J. E. Sparrow, Stewart Squires, Peter Stephens, Roland Taylor, Malcom Tudor, Suzanne Vaulkhard, Madge Wallhead, Duncan J. Walters, George Webdill, Mrs Georgina White, George Wilkinson, Carol Woodcock, and June Yeomans.